Reflections on
LEADERSHIP SUCCESS

Leo Anthony Kiesewetter

Copyright © 2015 Leo Anthony Kiesewetter

All rights reserved. No part of this book may be reproduced in any form without written permission from the author.

Cover photograph: WDG Photo/Shutterstock

ISBN: 1505301505

ISBN 13: 978-1505301502

Printed by CreateSpace

This book is dedicated to the many business and management instructors who have devoted their lives to the better understanding of the fundamentals that underlie management theories and practices, and more specifically, to individuals who encourage students to think on their own and formulate their own beliefs and philosophies. Each teacher brings a unique perspective to the classroom. With an open mind, a person can put together thoughts that eventually will create his or her own set of beliefs. Doing so makes for a well-rounded, productive person. It is to these many unheralded teachers that this book is dedicated.

Table of Contents

Acknowledgments 3

Preface 5

Introduction: Defining the Parameters 9

Chapter One: Management Styles 13

Chapter Two: Delegation of Authority 21

Chapter Three: Control 29

Chapter Four: Sources of Power 35

Chapter Five: Effective Communication 41

Chapter Six: Discipline 49

Chapter Seven: Motivation 57

Chapter Eight: Perception and Stress 65

Conclusion 73

About the Author 75

Acknowledgments

The formulation of my beliefs and theories of management resulted from many facets of my life. This process entailed the accumulation of knowledge and the synchronizing of thoughts from various readings and experiences over the course of my life. Even though many of my values and philosophies pertaining to management practices—or perhaps all of them—cannot be attributed to one specific person, the ideas and suggestions of others have profoundly affected me. Certainly the psychologists Frederick Herzberg, Elton Mayo, and Abraham Maslow offered some thought-provoking theories and ideas. But these theorists and others like them encourage individuals to foster their own lines of thinking. The brain must be stimulated and active, not rigid and passive.

It was my privilege to manage a large business department at Illinois Central College under the guidance of Dr. Svob, who gave me the reins to practice what I was teaching in the classroom. This included the delegation of authority, disciplining (including both positive and negative situations), goal setting for the department, and other such management practices. The most important of these would probably be the delegation of authority. With the ability to delegate, many other functions of a leader fall into place, such as providing motivation stimuli. This experience helped me organize, formulate, and solidify my philosophies regarding management.

These experiences and readings came into play while I wrote this book. Many thanks are due to all the people who were influential in shaping my thoughts regarding leadership and management that are reflected in the following pages.

As with my other books, Dena McDonald did a beautiful, professional job designing the book's interior and incorporating symbolism into the planning and designing the book's cover. Her dedication and thoroughness were exemplary.

Preface

Reflections on Leadership Success is drawn from my many experiences, studies, readings, and discussions over numerous years in education and business. Forty-some years in these fields have given me the opportunity to synchronize all of this information and formulate my thoughts regarding how leaders can be most successful in managing people.

Both sound and unproductive management practices can be found in successful and unsuccessful businesses. Some companies succeed despite their leadership. In other companies leaders try to make the right decisions but are stymied at almost at every juncture. After making suggestions and recommendations, many leaders become discouraged when they face repeated rejections. This causes some good leaders to leave the company, and others simply become zombies and put in their time.

In this book I attempt to cut through many of the theories and opinions presented in various forums to better define which path leads to successful leadership. In this analysis I also address and put to rest some myths. I do not hesitate to discuss any issue in this field, popular or not, in order to present the golden nuggets that form a productive leadership path. This would include the myth that the best way to do something is the way it has always been done. Or, it might be the idea that everything must be spelled out in a company policy book and nothing should deviate from that. Hopefully, the reader will find other management practices (myths) with which he or she can identify.

In this book, you will experience different aspects of leadership, which will affect whether or not a person is successful. To that end, there is a discussion of various elements of leadership that leaders encounter on a regular basis. The discussion includes, but is not limited to, such factors as different forms of and effective communication, motivational description and techniques, perception and how it affects interpersonal behavior, and concerns relating to leadership success.

It is not only important to understanding these factors; people in positions of leadership need to regularly and consistently implement them into productive practices. While reading this book, you will have a chance to evaluate your role as a current leader, an aspiring leader, or one who holds decision-making responsibilities in the hiring of leaders.

If you are one who makes hiring decisions for your business or organization, you will be given some guidelines to help identify the applicants who have the best chance to succeed. Upon completion of this book, you will be able to understand and more quickly recognize potential and some of the qualities of a good, effective leader.

Therefore, it is critically important that those who evaluate applications and resumés and interview candidates for leadership positions understand for themselves the characteristics of successful leaders. It is too costly for a business not to factor into its hiring practices all the information available. Cultivating successful leaders from *qualified* candidates is challenging enough. It is best to remove some of the challenges to your leadership training by selecting candidates from the very start who demonstrate potential. As this book explains, it will prevent setting up an unqualified candidate for failure, and your business will have a greater chance to succeed and be profitable.

Introduction
Defining the Parameters

"Under the guise of being fair, people try to make unequal things equal." This is a statement I wrote that hung in my office when I was the business department chairperson at the college where I was employed. It was a reminder to myself and others to approach decisions regarding personnel in a sound, productive manner. Fair is a word that's used and abused too frequently. It's a four-letter word that should be put to rest. All too often it's used as an excuse or, to be more direct, as a way for a leader to avert attention or criticism for a business decision he or she has made. The manager conveniently goes to the little "black book"—the policy manual—to address a particular problem "fairly." Nobody would ever dare go against the black book. In this way the policy manual too frequently becomes a rules manual. I discuss this subject in greater detail later in this book, but suffice it to say, there's an enormous difference between a policy manual and a rules manual, and this difference profoundly impacts how leaders manage people. A policy manual provides guidance, whereas a rules manual provides direction. When a leader uses a rules manual, he or she may have an easy way out.

While I'm on the subject of four-letter words, the word boss also should be discarded from the business vocabulary. The implication of the word is what makes it frustrating—it leaves the impression that there's only one style of management. The word "boss" seems to give the impression of one who tells and not one who confers with others in making decisions. When it is thought of like that, it gives credence to the autocratic style of management. Under these circumstances, a person would look to the leader "boss" for direction instead of thinking through the decision making process on his or her own. Later in this book, I discuss ways in which leaders manage.

Many factors contribute to a successful business. Some of them are difficult to control, and others probably can't be changed, but many of the ways leaders manage people can be effectively structured to provide a business the best chance for success.

These are the primary issues I discuss in this book. Hopefully *Reflections on Leadership Success* will help some businesses turn the corner and others become more productive. There aren't any guarantees when it comes to the structuring of management within any operation. The successful path I present in this book is based on my experiences in business as well as my many years of studying and teaching. History is something from which we learn, especially so we won't keep repeating the same errors.

Since this isn't a textbook, the discussion will be direct and to the point. The material is presented as food for thought. For some this book will provide a chance to reevaluate how they are leading. Even if just one thought can be taken from this book, it will be well worth a person's time and effort.

I don't attempt to teach facts in this book. Instead I give insight into how to lead people effectively. Once you learn how to lead people, you can do so regardless of the type of business situation in which you might find yourself.

The following is a statement I created that also appeared in my office: "To achieve all that is possible, attempt the impossible. To be as much as one can be, dream of being more."

CHAPTER 1

Management Styles

WHEN ASKED TO LIST various management styles, many people think of traditional, textbook styles. Usually the replies will be "autocratic," "democratic," "participative," and perhaps "laissez-faire." In general an autocratic leader makes all the key decisions, while a democratic organization is one in which a vote or consensus is obtained from workers regarding a decision a leader then makes. Under the participative style, a leader reviews workers' suggestions and recommendations then makes his or her decision. Lastly a laissez-faire organization doesn't have any formal management structure—probably mostly in theory. The French words basically mean the workers are left alone to do anything they want. Under this arrangement style the leader is there to make sure the workers have the necessary information and resources to be able to accomplish their goals. It would require highly motivated workers. This style might lend itself to a very unique situation in which there are a lot of individual aspects of the work.

Understanding each of these styles isn't bad for general discussion. In actual practice, however, it can be difficult to define a business's management style using only one of these descriptors. This is because in many situations it would appear that companies are using a mixture of the various styles. Yet, it is usually possible to ascertain the style in which any one company is favoring.

An individual's personality influences the way he or she manages. To a certain extent, this is acceptable as long as one's ego doesn't interfere with what should be the most productive way in which to carry out his or her work. Blending personality traits with management practices isn't always an easy process. If a person has been very domineering from early on, he or she may have difficulty straying from an autocratic management style.

It isn't uncommon for managers to follow in the footsteps of the people who previously managed them. In fact that's the reason some companies hire out of their organization to fill job openings. They feel that doing so will help bring in fresh ideas and new perspectives. Quite frequently hiring from within is referred to as "inbreeding."

A key question is whether it's possible to be successful using any of these leadership methods. The quick answer is yes. But there is more to this question than a quick answer. If being

> **THE POINT**
> In today's society workers probably despise the autocratic leadership style the most. They simply don't want to be left out of the decision-making process.

successful means being profitable, a general answer of yes might suffice. Here is where many companies fail. Instead of aiming to be profitable, a company should be tested on whether it's as productive as it can be. If a company can be 10 percent more productive, a merely profitable manager may be a liability to the organization.

Regardless of the style being used, there are times when a manager must be flexible. During an emergency situation, for example, a participative manager may not be able to wait for input but must make an immediate decision.

If a person is an autocratic leader, he or she can use some methods to soften the hard-nosed impression this management style sometimes suggests. For example the leader should fully explain all decisions to all persons concerned. This way everyone will know what to expect. Of course not everyone may agree with every decision, but at least they won't be left in the dark. People never should be left uninformed and uncertain as to what the company is planning; communication is paramount in any organization. I discuss this topic in more detail later in the book.

In today's society workers probably despise the autocratic leadership style the most. They simply don't want to be left out of the decision-making process. But this style is the easiest way to manage, which is why many managers succumb to it. In a way one might say it's the lazy way. Similarly straight lecturing in the classroom is the easiest, safest way to teach. Yet studies have indicated students learn more when they're actively involved in the learning process. Simply referring to the little "black book" (the policy manual) and stating what will be done is a "fail-safe" strategy for individuals who are managing a staff. This method is "fail-safe" because if anyone questions a decision, the manager can refer the worker to the manual then indicate that nothing can be done about it. Basically whatever happens is the manual's fault. In a classroom in which a teacher lectures, this particular delivery method of the subject matter generally discourages questions. This allows the teacher to feel safe, as he or she may not know the answer to a question that might be posed if questions from students were encouraged. As with autocratic managing, however, sometimes the best approach to teaching is the lecturing style. Restrictions regarding time and the subject matter being presented might dictate the delivery system on any particular day.

In general the most productive method of leadership is the participative style, sometimes called the consultative approach. This style is a takeoff of what once was called the democratic leadership style. The reason it is usually the most productive is because of the active participation of the workers. Participation happens to be one of the most effective stimuli to motivation.

Regardless of the type of management style one uses, it's important to have a proper span of management control. It might seem cost-effective to keep increasing the number of people a single individual supervises, but at some point, it will be counterproductive. First, there isn't any one number of employees that fits every circumstance. It's important to consider various factors, including the type of work, the personalities of the workers and their education levels, and the workplace layout, just to name a few.

Effective leaders prioritize the various jobs to be done. Poor leaders, on the other hand, may not address—or at least may not effectively address—tasks that are lower on their lists. This, in turn, may lead to additional stress experienced by these leaders and cause other problems such as fatigue, irritability, rudeness, shortness of temper, lack of sociability, and possibly leading to excessive drinking. This stress may come about when leaders feel it's necessary to spend more hours themselves to finish some of the work.

The span of management is extremely important and should not be taken lightly. If not addressed correctly, it could very likely cause less productivity, dissatisfied workers, stress on the part of the leader and workers, lack of proper and effective communication, and other such factors.

What is the ideal size of management? This is a good question but difficult to answer. Certainly the type of work should be considered. If the work requires highly educated people who will be working mostly on their own, the span might be somewhat larger. Then there is the experience and ability of the leader. Some can effectively manage more than another. If the span is too large, there probably will be signs such as a disgruntled worker, poor communication, and lack of motivational evidence.

CHAPTER 2

Delegation of Authority

THE DELEGATION OF AUTHORITY is one of the most difficult aspects of leadership. Many leaders tend to make very basic decisions that are better left to employees to make. One of the many reasons for this is the fear that someone else will make a mistake. This can cause a multitude of problems and concerns. Many times a leader will spend an undue amount of time at work, sometimes into the wee hours of night. In this person's mind, the only individual who can do the job right is him or her. Working long hours may create a great deal of stress for the leader, both at work and at home. He or she more than likely will be tired at work and tired and frustrated at home. By not delegating, the leader often finds that he or she overlooks or misses some other important matters.

After a leader gives an employee the authority to make decisions, it isn't uncommon for the employee to ask for directions when encountering a problem. Most of the time, the employee simply doesn't want to do something wrong. A leader must be very careful when addressing a situation such as this. The easy way out is to give the person the advice he or she requests. Although doing this makes some leaders look strong and powerful, it won't build confidence in the employee. In fact it undoubtedly will influence an employee to come back again when facing another problem. It's far more productive to return the question to the individual by asking him or her to explain what he or she might do to resolve the problem. Then the leader should let the person discuss his or her hesitancy. The usual answer will be that the employee is afraid of failure. The leader should ask what is the worst thing that could happen if the situation doesn't work out quite right. Then the discussion should explore the alternatives. Once, when discussing possible solutions to a problem with me, an employee responded, "Really? You mean I can actually do that?" From that day on, his performance was exemplary. It certainly appeared this gave him the confidence to make decisions and not worry about the possibility of things going wrong. You could almost feel the strength in his thoughts and his work.

During interviews for a leadership position in your company, try not to rely entirely on what an applicant is saying. It's extremely important to find out in the interview how the applicant performed in his or her previous leadership positions and how he or she delegated work in previous leadership roles. It's very easy at times for an applicant just to give the so-called correct answer. One effective way to determine a person's thought process is to give him or her a situational question. In many cases this will indicate how the applicant feels and would respond in that situation. It is interesting that at times after giving some dialog on the question, the applicant would ask if the response they gave was correct.

Equally important is for the applicant to ask questions regarding how the company feels about the delegation process. If the applicant doesn't express much curiosity about—or interest in—the company's delegation process, it might be a sign that in previous positions the person simply followed what was outlined for him or her and didn't make any substantial decisions relating to delegation.

Sometimes a leader is pressed for time and believes a task will get done faster if he or she does it. The style of leadership involved will dictate whether this occurs. If the company applies a restrictive, autocratic style, it will not delegate many decisions to employees; in other words almost everything will flow from the top down.

A leader may feel strongly that his or her employees do not have the ability to make reasonable and correct decisions. He or she may feel there's always the risk that something will go wrong if employees are allowed to make decisions.

Will the leader give credit where credit is due? This is another critical aspect of management, one that ties directly into the motivation of employees. (I discuss employee recognition in chapter seven.) Giving credit to others also ties into power, which I discuss in chapter four. Who should get credit for a job well done, and who should take the blame when things go wrong?

To ensure effective delegation of authority, certain steps must be taken. The first is to hire people who can make decisions. As previously mentioned, situational questions during an interview will provide some valuable insight as to how a person will make decisions. It might be questionable if the person responds that he or she would seek the advice of the leader of the unit. Also, it might be helpful to ask the person how it would feel if something didn't go quite right. Too often the wrong people are hired then fail because of their lack of experience or skills. This also applies to discipline, which I discuss in chapter six. Well placed and highly motivated people will cause fewer employee problems, such as reporting late, taking unusually long lunch breaks, abusive behavior, and the like. If the right people are in place, delegation will work much more smoothly. When the right people are hired, there is less chance of employee problems.

Another situation that could cause problems and lead to wrong decisions occurs when a leader communicates poorly. When workers are unaware of what is expected of them, it very likely will lead to confusion and stress. This could be due to a lack of communication skills or a fear of divulging the relevant information. Either way poor communication skills often lead to failure.

> **THE POINT**
> Regardless of who makes the decision, the leader is ultimately accountable, as is summed up in the old saying "The buck stops here."

Lastly, communication must be ongoing. An effective leader should give encouragement and recognition as a project is being accomplished. Doing so gives the person working on the project the opportunity to discuss any unusual situations that may arise.

One more underlying problem has a profound impact on this delegation process. It's the hidden reason many managers fail to delegate or sense the risk and fear involved with opening up with sensitive information or any information. The control of information is a major source of power in many leaders' mind. In management, accountability cannot be delegated. Regardless of who makes the decision, the leader is ultimately accountable, as is summed up in the old saying "The buck stops here."

Many leaders are consciously or subconsciously confused by the difference between delegation and the assignment of responsibilities. In most cases an assignment never should be given without a corresponding delegation of authority. This is necessary in order to have a smoothly run organization and, perhaps more important, create an atmosphere in which the greatest amount of benefits can be realized from the expertise of all people involved in the business.

In summary, to delegate effectively, a leader must hire the right people, speak and listen with open lines of communication, believe delegated tasks will be properly and effectively completed, and most important, let employees know he or she has confidence in them. Finally a decision or choice never should be between a right and a wrong but always between two rights. A situation never should arise in which one of the options is unethical or illegal—all options being considered should be appropriate.

Control

THIS CHAPTER EXAMINES sources of control and the ways in which control is used, as well as some misuses of it. Almost invariably, when there's a group of people, someone will want to control the flow of the discussion. That alone may present a big enough problem, but it becomes a much larger issue when more than one person in the group wants control. In past group conversations, you most likely will recall experiencing such a situation. This can become very uncomfortable when someone not only wants to control the entire discussion but also wants to convey that he or she has all the right answers.

But first what are the sources of control? Most sources are equally applicable to all business settings as well as informal social activities. Some sources can be applied verbally as well as nonverbally. One's tone of voice is sometimes used more frequently than is realized to control a conversation, especially if a person has a somewhat lower-toned voice coupled with a higher decibel. This voice may drown out the voices of others and may be perceived as very domineering. This individual's voice may discourage the sharing of ideas from other members of the group. People also may feel left out or shut down and become less likely to share ideas if their voices literally can't be heard. Ultimately this can hinder effective collaboration.

Some people are information seekers and thrive on having others look up to them for the information they have. Ineffective business leaders use their information to maintain control over the people they lead. Some people also do this manipulatively in social gatherings when they wish to keep others in suspense and hold the attention of a group.

Intentionally making people wait is another technique some leaders use to maintain control. Even if making others wait isn't intentional, it will have an effect on others. A good example of this is when someone goes to a manager's office—or for that matter, anyone's office or desk—and isn't immediately acknowledged. The longer one waits, the more control the other party generates. This might make a person feel intimidated, and, subsequently when the person finally has a meeting with the leader, he or she may feel stressed and inferior. Any such meeting probably will be ineffective.

> **THE POINT**
>
> Some people are information seekers and thrive on having others look up to them for the information they have. Ineffective business leaders use their information to maintain control over the people they lead.

What lessons can be learned from this? A leader must understand interpersonal relationships and communication so that he or she doesn't create a negative, unproductive work environment. Therefore he or she must use control in a complimentary, respectful manner. As mentioned, even a leader's tone of voice can cause uncertainty and negative feelings in others. There are times when sensitive, confidential information must be withheld, but this shouldn't be done to demonstrate superiority, and it certainly shouldn't be done as a means to maintain discipline. This also applies to making someone wait. If a leader is busy, he or she should at least make a quick acknowledgment. Again a leader shouldn't make employees wait so that he or she can establish discipline.

The subject of control leads neatly to the subject of power, which I discuss in the next chapter.

CHAPTER 4
Sources of Power

Sources of Power

POWER IS CLOSELY RELATED to control. The following discussion pertains primarily to sources of power as well as the misuse of power. As with many factors in leadership, power can be used effectively, or it can be detrimental to one's goal of having extremely productive employees.

Power can be separated into primary and secondary sources. Primary sources include money, information, education, and prestige. Secondary sources include intimidation, fear, and job status.

Sometimes a person inadvertently or intentionally creates a power situation. Here is where the leader is exerting influence by being portrayed as someone above the workers. This typically is done by leveraging secondary sources of power, such as creating fear in employees or intimidating them. If a leader senses that employees feel afraid or intimidated, it could influence his or her behavior. The leader's response could provide a pleasant, receptive environment or a distrustful and uncertain situation. As chairperson of the department, it was my practice to defuse the inherent power that my office setting may have presented. I visited with faculty members as often as possible in their offices. Not only did they appreciate this, but it also made for a more relaxed atmosphere.

Many people are in awe when they interact with someone who is wealthy. And it isn't unusual for the person with money to use the awe of others in order to wield power over them. In a social group, this person very likely may become the spokesperson of the group or the leader of its conversation or activities.

Information is tied into the delegation process. When a person receives authority to carry out a task, information is passed on to this person. It can be easy for a leader to use this

> **THE POINT**
> Power can be used positively or negatively. It must be applied in a way that ensures the best possible atmosphere in a business and supports increased productivity.

dynamic as a source of power. The worker perceives that the leader has this power because of the information he or she has. Basically, the leader can either give out the information or withhold it. This could be very powerful.

In addition people have a natural tendency to admire someone with an education or someone who has made significant achievements, whether in sports, politics, entertainment, or any other field. People who fall into these categories often possess power as a result of their achievements.

The misuse of power can have a profound impact on interpersonal relationships within a company. Rather than a leader, a person becomes a dictator. At least that's what the perception often may be. Sometimes leaders overuse power in the form of forced discipline. This may be when a leader implies or explicitly states that a person's job evaluation is in jeopardy or his or her job itself might be on the line. Leaders like this will often use intimidation to keep people in line. If an individual's power is very evident, it can negatively affect proper communication within a business, which can lead to poor performance or the misinterpretation of directives.

In summary power can be used positively or negatively. It must be applied in a way that ensures the best possible atmosphere in a business and supports increased productivity. It's unfortunate that delegation and power are so badly misunderstood. Many leaders fail to delegate because they believe doing so means relinquishing authority or power. Actually the reverse is true—the more a leader effectively delegates, the more powerful he or she becomes. In order to delegate, a person must have the authority to do so, which makes him or her a powerful person by the nature of the process.

Often power dynamics can be softened somewhat through proper communication, which I discuss in the next chapter.

CHAPTER 5
Effective Communication

COMMUNICATION IS BOTH verbal and nonverbal. In this chapter I discuss oral and written communication first then offer some thoughts on nonverbal communication.

Verbal communication

It might sound contradictory, but for one to be effective in business, discussions should be brief yet inclusive. This means you need to leave out the fluff. At times so many conversational tangents may arise that the entire point of the discussion is lost. People may lose focus, become distracted, and possibly tune out. The message must be brief and to the point. Yet it can't be so brief that important information is left out. Being concise often is a fine line to walk, but doing so is important. When a speaker notices people beginning to squirm, or when eye contact is lost, it's time to make adjustments. This is true whether the person is leading a round-table discussion or giving a speech to an audience. Whatever the setting, the speaker should look for signs of understanding. I discuss nonverbal communication in greater detail in the second part of this chapter.

Especially in a group discussion setting, using the "in-and-out" approach is a sound practice and is appropriate for either a small or large group. A person should say what is pertinent then let another person contribute—in other words leave out unnecessary details. It can be extremely uninteresting and time consuming when someone takes over a conversation by making irrelevant comments. Just remember, what you're saying is already known by you, but what someone else says might be new to you. Therefore listening is just as important as speaking.

Regardless of the setting, one must use the language best understood by the people involved. The level of conversation shouldn't be appreciably above or below the understanding level of the audience. Remember, it's the listeners you're trying to reach, and they must feel comfortable. Therefore stay away as much as you can from using the word I. Instead try to use the word you as much as possible. This, in general, makes others feel important. Even when leaders are addressing a number of people, they should try to use the word I as infrequently as possible.

What are some things a leader should be cognizant of when planning and conducting a meeting? First, have a precise agenda. The agenda shouldn't be merely a list of items to discuss but also should include a brief statement about each item. Try to steer

> **THE POINT**
> A person should say what is pertinent then let another person contribute—in other words leave out unnecessary details.

away from the notion that everyone should be surprised by what you have to say. Also refrain from withholding information as a means to derive power, as discussed in chapter four.

After a departmental meeting, a teacher came to my office to question a communication sent to the faculty. Because I had properly composed an agenda from a previous meeting, it was easy for me to refer back to it and address the situation with the teacher. I answered his question, and he left feeling positive about the interaction.

Beginning a meeting with a pertinent statement to get everyone's attention is often an effective technique. This should be done in the context of what has been written in regard to the agenda item. The statement can even be humorous.

Lastly look for feedback from the group. This can include verbal or nonverbal communication. If necessary, ask a few questions to make sure everyone understands the key points of the discussion.

Nonverbal communication

One doesn't need to be an expert to recognize some of the basics of nonverbal communication. A productive leader should not only recognize nonverbal actions but also understand how some of these actions can be interpreted effectively when he or she is supervising people. Actually, at times, people who are being supervised can improve their quality of work by applying sound nonverbal methods. Therefore this discussion applies to leaders as well as employees.

The seating around a table, for example, can be important. Many times there will be a definite head of the table, which is a power position. If a leader wants to neutralize his or her power, he or she should take a different seat. If showing power is important, he or she should sit at the head of the table.

The seat immediately to the left or right of the power seat also is usually considered important. Regardless of the design of the table, the seat in which one's back is to the door is usually the uncomfortable one. Again if a leader is trying to neutralize the power dynamic, he or she should take a seat that allows the other participants to feel at ease.

A leader should be aware of the personal space of others. Being too close to someone—in other words encroaching upon his or her personal space—may make an individual feel quite uncomfortable and will hinder effective communication. In general how well two people know each other determines the boundaries of personal space. The imaginary circle around a person becomes smaller as the relationship becomes more personal and as the friendship grows. Just think of a crowded elevator—can you recall how uncomfortable it is to be so close to strangers in a confined space?

If the leader is tall, he or she might want to downplay his or her height—yet another power indicator—by sitting down. Again if the leader wishes to display power, he or she should stand. The leader's desk also may be a factor. If the leader wants to defuse the power that his or her desk may imply, he or she can sit someplace else in the room. At a minimum it's important to offer others seats at each side of the desk, which will help create a much more conversational setting.

As mentioned in chapter three, a leader's tone of voice is also important. A loud voice can be intimidating and may trigger responses that are equally loud. In general many disagreements get out of hand because people return loud responses and comments. A leader can control this by staying even keel.

Using a loud tone of voice is like a trap that people set. This is also true with written communication; a harsh letter or e-mail often is followed by a harsh reply.

Whether it is a one-on-one setting or a group meeting arrangement, the leader should be able to determine the interest of the people involved. Certainly, one of the most important indicators is eye contact. If this is lacking, it is very possible the message of the leader is not registering with his or her audience. Other factors might be the uneasiness of the people shown by constant moving about in their chair and the lack of questions asked when given the opportunity. A powerful opening statement by the leader can overcome some of this.

In summary, as a leader, know what you want to accomplish when you're communicating. It's also important to know your audience. Make sure you use power in the most productive manner. Certainly do not misuse your power when communicating. Above all, realize the importance of understanding and respecting interpersonal relations in business settings.

CHAPTER 6

Discipline

THE WORD DISCIPLINE often conjures negative images. It implies sanctions or some type of punishment. It's far more effective, however, to think in terms of positive discipline. I realize those may sound like contradictory words. Another way of saying "positive discipline" is "preventive discipline." This is a process of establishing an atmosphere in which problems will be at a minimum.

For a business to be productive and successful, the right people must be hired. Applicants who aren't a good fit can be identified in a number of ways. If an applicant doesn't possess the necessary skills to perform the various tasks the job requires, there will be a problem in the waiting. A person with a poor résumé or mediocre personal references also is a potential problem. If the person was a troublemaker elsewhere, there's a good chance he or she will be again. So the first order of business is to hire the right people.

After that a proper motivational system must be in place. An unmotivated person is just waiting in the wings to present problems. I discuss motivational techniques in the next chapter.

Every employee must be well informed about what the company expects. It's difficult—and counterproductive—to blame someone who doesn't know the company's guidelines.

Another aspect of discipline that frequently is overlooked is the misunderstanding that occurs when there's lack of clarity between what a policy is and what a rule is. These differences between a policy and rule were discussed in the introduction.

An ineffective manager—or even a poorly designed management structure—encourages the use of policies as rules. Undoubtedly numerous companies treat policies as rules when in fact these policies are guidelines for leaders to use when making decisions. Conversely situations arise in which a policy should be considered a rule or a policy rule. Regardless a rule is something that must be implemented. For example federal, state, and local regulations and laws are mandatory and must be enforced by company leaders. This might include safety regulations that require wearing a certain type apparel; such as, safety shoes or safety glasses. Also, these regulations might include hiring methods and procedures.

But other policies should be treated as guidelines for leaders to use while making decisions. For example this might be a policy regarding a company dress code. If the clothing employees wear isn't crucial to their jobs—as it is in the case of military personnel or police officers—then the company's dress code should be considered a policy rather than a rule. So, when it does not fall into the rule category, as explained, the leader has some discretion when an exception must be made, This might be a temporary situation when a worker has incurred an injury which would make it difficult for him or her to wear the prescribed clothing.

Many leaders believe that using a policy as a rule helps make decisions about disciplining much easier. On the surface it probably does. By treating a policy as a rule, the leader merely consults the little "black book" to find the listed disciplinary sanction. Then, if there's a disagreement, the leader shows the employee the so-called required punishment. In the long run, however—and sometimes even in the short term—treating a policy as a rule can create problems. The most important thing is the perception it might cause with workers who feel a leader does not have much authority to act on his or her own. Secondly,

> **THE POINT**
> If an applicant doesn't possess the necessary skills to perform the various tasks the job requires, there will be a problem in the waiting.

it indicates the important thing is that it looks equal in the beginning and not on the final outcome. Does the decision made affect all parties the same in the final analysis? That would be the most important question.

In reality there should be very few rules. Rather leaders should follow policies, meaning guidelines they can use to reflect upon when they're deciding on the proper action they should take in a given situation. Doing this implies that each event is different and must be treated as such. No two people are the same, and no two events are the same, even if it's only a matter of when the event takes place—for example February versus September or morning versus afternoon.

At this point the word fair undoubtedly will be heard. As mentioned in this book's introduction, this word should be taken out of the dictionary and permanently retired. First of all it's most frequently used at the beginning of an action. If used at all, the word fair should be used when measuring end results. Here's an example. If two people get into a fight at work, the little "black book" might dictate that the individuals must be suspended for three days without pay. On the surface this may sound fair to both individuals. Well, it so happens that one of the two people enjoys hunting, and the days off coincide with the opening of deer-hunting season. He or she might take these days as a vacation and be pleased with the time off. In fact the employee might have been ready to ask for the time off even before the incident occurred. The other person, on the other hand, is barely making it financially. The three days without pay might create a terrible financial situation for him or her. In this situation is the leader being fair? Remember, the end results are what should matter. As I mentioned, however, various regulations and laws must be considered. All this certainly underscores that managing employees can be difficult, and effective management requires effective leaders.

Is finding the right balance easy to accomplish? The answer is no. In leadership the right thing to do is often the most difficult and requires a person with sound management skills to do it correctly.

While I was taking corrective action with two teachers in different situations, one of them accepted a recommendation and made the necessary changes. In the other case, the teacher was reluctant to understand the problem and was disturbed by the accusation. But when I fully explained the repercussions if he didn't make the necessary changes, he acquiesced. Even though he was reluctant, he understood the problem and the steps he needed to take to resolve it.

Who is this "right leader"? A person who understands correct managerial duties and has the ability to perform them is the right leader. Does the prospective leader understand motivational techniques, styles of leadership, rules and policies, disciplinary procedures, and other such factors discussed in this book? Too often the wrong person is hired for a leadership position. One must remember that managing people is different from being an accountant or a salesperson. Being the most productive person in either of these two fields does not in and of itself make someone a good leader. For example the best baseball player on the field will not necessarily be the best team manager.

So, when filling a leadership position, one must look for an individual who possesses superb managerial skills and not just the best sales or accounting skills.

If the right people are hired, the chances of a company having personnel problems are sharply reduced. A phrase I mention in the introduction to this book summarizes this chapter on discipline: "Under the guise of being fair, people try to make unequal things equal."

CHAPTER 7
Motivation

SOME OF MY THOUGHTS and feelings regarding motivation were gleaned from the writings of Frederick Herzberg, Abraham Maslow, and Elton Mayo. These psychologists were very cognizant of individuals' inner feelings and how people respond to leaders. By studying the works of these three gentlemen as well as other writings, a foundation can be formed regarding how motivation is intertwined with leadership. A leader who isn't familiar with the basics of motivation will have difficulty effectively managing people.

Let's get one thing straight from the beginning. A human being cannot be motivated. Certain stimuli, however, can be applied that may cause a person to be in a motivated state. This is because motivation comes from the inside; it is internal. Some individuals use the word motivation believing it comes from external factors. Regardless it's important to understand what spurs people to be in a motivated state (i.e., external stimuli) and when a person is in a motivated state that will produce positive results. Motivation is one of the most difficult factors to understand, as is the ability to apply the stimuli at the right time and under the proper conditions.

Motivation pertains to a way a person feels; therefore it is an internal factor. A number of conditions contribute to getting people activated from within. These conditions can be separated into two basic groups. There are external factors (or nonsatisfiers), and there are stimuli that may cause a change in one's feelings. Nonsatisfiers include money, working conditions, style of management, office layout, benefits, pleasant surroundings, and other external factors. Stimuli that may cause motivation include recognition, assignment of responsibility, accomplishment, praise, advancement, and other similar factors.

When I asked students in my classes what the most important motivator for them was, almost always 100 percent

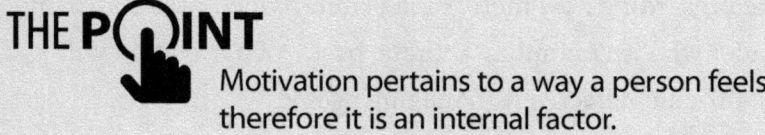

THE POINT
Motivation pertains to a way a person feels; therefore it is an internal factor.

of them indicated money. Yes, I did expect this answer. I then told them that after the completion of the unit, very few if any of them would give the same response. And almost always there was a 100 percent change in their answers at the end of the course.

Oh! But this seems contrary to human nature. I agree. On the surface money seems to be what people would call a motivator. Let's make this a little more confusing. Even though money isn't a motivator, it's probably the most important overall factor involved in a person's motivation. Well, hopefully by the end of this chapter, things will be a little clearer.

How about the following statement? A dissatisfied person cannot be in a state of motivation. As money is probably the most important nonsatisfier, a person who's dissatisfied with his or her salary probably won't react to a motivational stimulus such as accomplishment, praise, or advancement. This is the reason many times one person happily displays a recognition plaque and can't wait to tell friends and relatives about it, whereas another person places it in a desk drawer or, in extreme cases, in the wastebasket. The first person is satisfied, while the second is dissatisfied by something—quite possibly money.

Why not just give a person more and more money? Interestingly, when a person's pay is increased, dissatisfaction about money often goes away, but when an individual has gone past the point of satisfaction, increased pay does not cause motivation. In other words if an individual needs an additional $100 a week to clear any dissatisfaction, giving him or her $200 a week will not cause true motivation.

The reason for this misunderstanding is probably due to the fact some leaders witness changes in employees when dissatisfaction about money is removed. There's no more unhappiness or bitterness about wages or salary. That's a change in feelings, however, and not motivation.

Even more confusion arises when one takes into account that the line between being satisfied and dissatisfied may constantly change. For example a person with a $100 salary deficiency may find out when he returns home one evening that his neighbor or brother was laid off without any money forthcoming from wages or salary. At that moment the $100 deficiency that made him dissatisfied disappears, and he feels fortunate that he still has a job. That's just one example. Many other conditions could cause the "satisfied/dissatisfied" line to change.

All of the discussion about motivation just underscores the necessity to hire a leader who has strong leadership skills. As I mentioned earlier, being an outstanding salesperson doesn't mean a person necessarily has leadership skills.

The question that might be posed is how this outstanding salesperson can be rewarded. Rewarding the person could involve giving him or her a more lucrative sales territory. If the person is promoted to a leadership position and doesn't have proper management skills, the firm will be hurt in two ways. First, the company will lose a top-notch salesperson, and second, it will have an ineffective, frustrated leader.

As an example I readily saw the enthusiasm (motivation) in a teacher when he accepted an assignment to explore and eventually bring to fruition an associate-degree program and concomitant new courses in his field of study.

Does this just mean giving up on all this motivational stuff? The answer is no. It means a good leader earns his or her pay. The important thing is that a leader understands motivation and all its ramifications.

In summary, in order to have a person in a motivated state, it is important to recognize whether or not the person is dissatisfied by something. In many situations this could be because of the amount of salary or wage involved. Once this or any other dissatisfaction is addressed and satisfied, then applying some of the factors or stimuli that foster the motivation from within can be applied. This would include such things as recognition, assignment of responsibilities, and other factors mentioned above.

CHAPTER 8
Perception and Stress

A LEADER'S PERSPECTIVE is extremely important when he or she is trying to understand the emotions an employee may have when confronted with an unpleasant situation. It isn't uncommon for two or more people viewing the same event to have different interpretations of what happened. If a leader doesn't approach the situation properly, friction and negative feelings may arise. An effective leader who understands perception and knows the value of interpersonal relations can defuse almost any discord and often transform it into something positive. Therefore, as previously mentioned, an organization must hire managers who understand how to effectively work with people.

Sadly some leaders either ignore friction that is festering among workers or aren't adept at observing these dynamics. The latter typically occurs when a leader simply functions behind his or her desk all day. Friction and discontent in a company almost always lead to increased stress among employees. I discuss the issue of stress later in this chapter.

It's important to remember that a person's perception is very real to him or her. Conflicting views or differing personal interpretations of an event can cause severe disruptions in a workplace. And the longer disagreements linger, the more anger, distrust, and separation occur, with a possible decrease in productivity and morale. In these cases a leader must apply proper methods and techniques to soften and resolve conflicts. If conflicts are left unaddressed, the productivity of the people involved certainly will decrease, which may affect the productivity of other employees as well.

One might ask how varying interpretations arise when two or more workers witness one set of circumstances. Well, it isn't that uncommon. Many times two people observe a conflict, and each person relates a different story.

What causes these different perceptions? Some reasons include past experiences, education, family background, money, and power. In business a person's past experiences with a certain type of leader might create a personal view of how to act or reply in a given situation. When coming from one company to another, even though the management structure isn't the same as it was in the previous company, the employee could very well believe certain behavior is expected. If the employee has held these beliefs for a many years, it might take a long time for his or her thought process to change.

Certainly an individual's level of education may influence the way in which he or she views a situation. For example a person with a college degree may more critically approach a situation and possibly incorporate more logic in regard to the facts presented. Education also could be a factor between two people with doctorate degrees who studied in different fields. For example an individual with a law degree may have a different perspective than a person with a PhD in English. These are factors an effective leader will keep in mind when addressing a disagreement between two or more workers.

It might be helpful if the leader is aware of the employees' family backgrounds. This will depend somewhat on whether employees are willing to share this information. Did one or more of the workers come from a difficult childhood? Or was everything given to him or her without much effort? Did the parents strictly discipline the child as he or she was growing up? I could enumerate many other factors here, but the point is that a person's childhood and upbringing may very well influence his or her perception. For example, a person who grew up under a very authoritative father and or mother might feel this is the way authority figures conduct themselves socially or in the work place. It could be that an employee did not receive much praise, recognition, or support from his or her parents, and this might be what they are looking for now.

Money and power can be interwoven into a person's frame of mind. An affluent person often has a different mind-set than a person with limited resources. In addition a person who has power—or perceives he or she has power—will probably view

THE POINT
It isn't uncommon for two or more people viewing the same event to have different interpretations of what happened.

a situation differently than someone who is very mild mannered or docile. In addition a person with a more aggressive or larger-than-life personality will view a situation differently than someone who is more mild mannered or docile. Again these factors may influence the way in which a person perceives a specific occurrence.

In one actual experience I faced, two female colleagues definitely saw a situation differently, and their feelings were quite evident to me. Knowing that this type of conflict and lack of communication wasn't healthy for them and the institution, I asked them to see me in my office. At the beginning of this conference, neither one looked at each other. I asked how each of them felt and how she viewed the conflict. As each woman explained her thoughts, the other looked puzzled. It seemed their relationship changed when one of them said, "I didn't know you felt that way." The conversation between the two went really well after that. As they left my office, they were enjoying a very encouraging conversation.

There isn't anything inherently wrong or negative about stress. What's important is how a person manages or controls stressful situations. In fact stress can be productive if properly managed. Certainly one can speculate that a person who's in a stressful environment and unable to manage it will have a different view or perception than someone who carefully and effectively manages the emotions triggered by stress. An effective manager will have the social awareness to pick up on nonverbal signs when asking questions and realize the differences in perception each person brings to the table. In a meeting I had with a teacher, it was clear that he was aware of a nonverbal expression I inadvertently was giving him. While I was looking down at my desk, reading some information that was pertinent to our conversation, the teacher felt I wasn't listening to him because of my lack of eye contact. This was a valid assumption and perception on his part. I, in fact, was listening to him, but that didn't matter, because he perceived I wasn't. As soon as I realized what was happening, I returned eye contact to immediately defuse the situation. There was no need for me to explain our differing perceptions at the time; as soon as I returned eye contact, our meeting turned out to be very productive.

A manager may want to recommend that an employee seek help outside the work environment to better understand stress and healthy ways to express and manage the emotions that result from stress. It isn't the goal of this chapter to discuss these methods; the goal is to emphasize that stress can influence the way a person views situations and events in the workplace.

As mentioned throughout this book, being an effective leader requires much more than being an excellent results-oriented employee (an accountant or a computer technician, for example). When one is hiring a leader for a management role, it's important to zero in on applicants' leadership skills. This doesn't mean an effective leader can't be found within an accounting or sales department; however, great skills don't always equate to effective leadership abilities.

How people see things—i.e., their perception—can affect relationships and lead to conflicts and ill feelings among coworkers. This discord may carry over to social events outside the workplace. An effective leader will be able to help each person understand the other party's interpretation of an event.

Once this happens, issues typically are resolved, and employees will be more cooperative and productive.

Conclusion

The previous chapters address various aspects of management as they pertain to leadership. It's sometimes difficult to ascertain effective leadership when the economy is buzzing and a company is making healthy profits. But reviewing and evaluating leadership should be an ongoing process and should be undertaken with the same vigor whether the economy is booming or tanking. Just because a company may have made a 10 percent profit in a certain year doesn't mean it has excellent leadership. With more effective management, the company may have enjoyed a 12 percent or 15 percent profit.

Throughout this book I've used the terms leadership and management. I didn't use both words to be confusing but to acknowledge that leadership is part of management and also to suggest that a leader is involved with many aspects of the management process. For example a leader often deals with budgetary issues. Managing work is different from leading people.

My thoughts and ideas in this book were gleaned from my many years in business and education. Even though I believe experiences cannot be taught, the knowledge from experience can be used to underscore principles and philosophies. When I was considering accepting the position of chairperson of the business department at a community college, it was important for me to hear the dean tell me I could manage the department according to the basic principles and practices I taught my students. To his credit (and I'll always be appreciative of this), he was very supportive and always encouraged these practices.

As mentioned this book isn't intended to be a textbook. It might be appropriate as a supplement in management classes. It also could be used to tie together the theories of a textbook and classroom teaching with actual practices in the business world.

Finally, if anyone has any aspiration of becoming a leader, it should be understood that being a leader is quite rewarding when it is performed in a productive, informative way. It is critical for people to enjoy what they are doing. If you think you might have the characteristics outlined in this book, then it behooves you to explore the possibility of being a leader.

Take the time to read, study, and take some classes that will help you enjoy working with and leading people. Read some of the writing of the people I mentioned in this book. They will provide you with a lot of food for thought. The company for whom you are working will appreciate your talent as a leader. May you have a successful career.

About the Author

Leo Anthony Kiesewetter holds a master's degree in business education and has completed postgraduate work in business.

He spent twenty-nine years as a teacher and administrator at the high school and college levels. For fourteen of these years, he was the chairperson of the department of business at Illinois Central College in East Peoria, Illinois. Before that he was an accountant for a real estate developer then owned his own real estate company. After high school he served two years in the Army.

As the chairperson of the department of business, Kiesewetter was responsible at one time or another for all aspects of the college's business programs. He also provided leadership for thirty-four full-time and 120 part-time faculty members. Owning a small real-estate company also provided him additional leadership experiences.

Kiesewetter has written and published three novels (*The Story of Love and the Missing Lara*, *The Murder of George*, and *The Vineyard Surprise*) as well as a book of poetry (*The Reflections of Poetry*).

www.ingramcontent.com/pod-product-compliance
Lightning Source LLC
Chambersburg PA
CBHW071757170526
45167CB00003B/1074